The Struggle Never Ends

Analyzing The Struggle; Preparing For Our Survival
by
Roger N. Toppin Sr.

Harriet Tubman

W.E.B. De Bois

Thurgood Marshall

Paul Robeson

Marcus Garvey

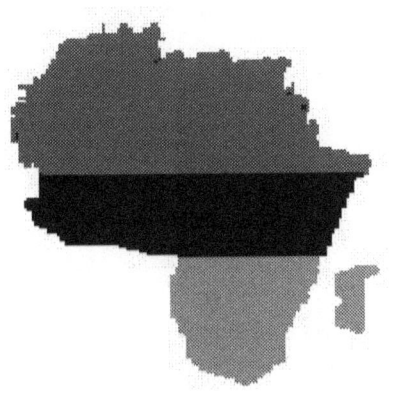

George Washington Carver

Martin Luther King Jr.

Malcom X (EI-Hajj Malik EI-Shabazz

authorHOUSE

1663 *LIBERTY DRIVE, SUITE* 200
BLOOMINGTON, INDIANA 47403
(800) 839-8640
www.authorhouse.com

First published by AuthorHouse 05/18/04

ISBN: 1-4184-1823-4 (e)
ISBN: 1-4184-1824-2 (sc)

Printed in the United States of America
Bloomington, IN

This book is printed on acid free paper.

TABLE OF CONTENTS

About the cover of "The Struggle Never Ends" designed by Roger T. Toppin Jr. (age 17)

SOME OF THE PEOPLE WHO WERE INVOLVED IN THE STRUGGLE

Harriet Tubman: was a great woman! Also known as "The Moses of her people" Who established and ran the Underground Railroad, which took many slaves to freedom. During the Civil War Tubman served as a nurse and spy for the Federal Army.

George Washington Carver: was a former slave who became an economic genius, helping America move forward economically by inventing over three hundred uses for the peanut and soybeans.

Marcus Garvey: platform was Blacks controlling their own businesses and the "Back to Africa Movement". He established the Negro Factories & The Black Star Line.

W.E.B. De Bois: was the first Black graduate from Harvard University.. One of his thesis was Blacks had two consciences one Black and one White. He was a former editor of NAACP *The Crisis* magazine.

Paul Robeson: was great at anything he did, which included politics, academics, sports, theater etc. He was way ahead of his time. He was well known as the actor in "Emperor Jones".

Malcolm X (El-Hajj Malik El-Shabazz): took the Race issue to the United Nations and made it an international issue. He was a persona non grata (not wanted around) until his unfortunate death, and then everyone wanted to relate to his beliefs and the letter X.

Martin Luther King Jr.: was a drum major for human rights and civil rights. He said one day people would not be judged by the color of their skin or their religion, but by the content of their character. He joined the Montgomery Boycott, which was successful, pushing America in a positive direction.

Thurgood Marshall: former Supreme Court Judge who made a difference on the highest court in the land. One of his cases was Brown vs. The Board of Education of Topeka (1954), which changed the whole American Educational System and made America a better country for everyone.

There are many more people who were involved in the STRUGGLE to many to mention in this book. We must give praise to everyone who helped move us forward and remember, "The Struggle Never Ends".

7-10-2001

OPENING STATEMENT

You have just become a part of the solution! After reading this book you will walk away with an open mind. You have taken the first step, which is recognizing the problem. The second step is working on the solution.

The objective of this book " The Struggle Never Ends" is to convey to America where we have been, where we are now and where we are going.

This book is also a blueprint for the next generation, who will be responsible for the next phase of the struggle.

I will be addressing some of Americas' problems, giving you some true to life scenarios; I will also be giving some recommended solutions.

We are all a part of the American experience; we must take part in its greatness and survival.

Please feel free to take part (communicate) as we travel this American journey of life, because "The Struggle Never Ends".

FOREWORD

This book is a Black perspective and a microcosm of the world we live in today. It was written to enlighten Black people in particular and everyone else in general. I had plan on writing a book for years, but procrastinated with excuses such as I do not have any money to publish it or I do not have any time to put it together and most importantly I was afraid that people would come after me for telling the truth. I feel I am at the stage and age of no return. It is very important to me to leave my mark in the sands of time. I will rest easier once this book is published and you have read my thoughts and maybe relate to some of the experiences that I talk about in this book, You are welcome to communicate with me because communications is a very important phase of learning and progress to move up to the next level. What some people say about me does not really matter now. I feel that it is very important to pass on a legacy to the next generation that is educational and positive after you have absorbed the contents of this book I think you will see that " The Struggle Never Ends".

Words of wisdom # 1: He who struggle and loses is always one step ahead of someone who did not struggle; engage their soul and freed their heart.

FOUNDATION

First I give thanks to God the almighty that blow life into my body and made it possible to travel the journey of life. I have been blessed to reach this phase of life, and to be able to pass on a document of experience to the next generation. It is very important that everyone study our history so that we can better understand the psychological chains placed on the minds of Blacks and other people, which is a continuation of slavery.

I recall reading something about WEB De Bois stating Blacks having two thoughts one white and one Black. If you want to survive you must never forget you are Black, For example look at some of the current headlines (August 2003) Superstar accused of raping a white girl he may get life; a Black man shot dead by police who believed a beer bottle was a gun; a Man who was dating a white girl in Belle Glade, Florida hung himself from a tree with his hands tied behind his back. I can go on and on but I hope I made a point that "The Struggle Never Ends".

ACKNOWLEDGEMENTS:

I give thanks to the following people; if I missed your name I apologize, please let me know so I will make sure you are included in the next book.

First I must give a special thank you to my good friend Estelle Ann Rollins who wrote the book " Precious Memories, Sharing Joy, Love and Lifelines A Family Reunion" her spirit and energy was instrumental in making me get off of my backside (smile), check out her book, www.1stBooks.com. to obtain your copy. My son Roger Toppin Jr. (age 17) who is a great writer, artist and proofreader and keeps me up to speed on what the young people are thinking. Thanks to my cousin Joyce who helped me out during by post marriage homeless days. My oldest son Eric and his wife Donna, we must ever forget for every successful person there is a support person or persons; Eric who is always giving me ideas on how to improve my writing style. Eric set a great example by finishing college, building a new home, getting a great job and raising his family in the Maryland community. On Tuesday, October 14, 2003, my son Eric's wife Donna gave birth to a baby boy named Jermaine. Hopefully one day the newborn will read this book and understand that "The Struggle Never Ends".

Thanks to my sister Carrie who is a super proofreader, she makes sure I dot every I and cross every T; she is the oldest Toppin in our family. Thanks to my Aunt Cleonis and my cousin John who helped me though my teen years in the Bronx and continues to support me today. Thanks to my goddaughter Delores (Penny) who always gives people good advise and stay in touch with everyone. Thanks to my uncle Revered Willis Bell, who build his own church with the help of his family, in Akien, South Carolina, his sister which was my Auntie Mildred Robinson who expired in 2003; she had five sons one was killed in the Korean war; she lived to be ninety nine years old, she was a strong independent Black women. Thanks to my cousin Arnold whose mother my late Aunt Leola would feed the family with her great holiday dinners. Thanks to my cousin Peggy who has always been involved in the Black struggle. All of the above family, friends and a lot of other people who I did not mention were instrumental in my survival and reaching this point in my life.

PEOPLE WHO INFLUENCED MY LIFE

1   Malcolm X (Shabazz), he took The Black dilemma to the United Nations.

2   Reverend, Martin Luther King Jr., He forced America to change for the better, but paid with his life.

3   Nelson Mandela, put almost 20 years in prison then came out to become the first Black President of South Africa.

4   Lyndon Banes Johnson, the late President of the United States of America, helped move America forward with his program of "The Great Society".

1   Reverend Al Sharpton, Spoke out on injustices when all the so call politicians were afraid to represent.

Reverend Calvin O. Butts, pastor of Abyssinian Baptist Church, implemented programs to up lift the Harlem and New York Community.

Ms. Cynthia Mc Kinney, former State Congress person, who dared to challenge President of the United States of

America actions or inactions, lost her seat as an elected official.

Reverend Calvin E. Owens, pastor of Community Protestant Church; who after years of struggle with the system; supported by his congregation built their own Church.

Reverends Ann L. and Thomas Palmore, Pastors of The Church of New Vision, who run several programs to up lift the souls of people in the community.

Reverend Shelton E. Williams, Pastor of the Co-op City Baptist Church, who has a special ministry for young men, which helps them prepare for the future.

Mr. Tony Illis, who is the President of The Black Forum and Current Riverbay Board of Director; he is legally blind, but he is smarter, very knowledgeable and more active than most people who live in the community. He has been on the forefront of fighting to keeping The Co-op City development in the Mitchell- Lama program, which translates to affordable housing for the people who remain and continue to live in the community.

12-24-00

Russa Skkirr

"WHY"

Why the struggle never ends.

Where there is life there will be struggle.

Where there is hope there is struggle.

Where there are proud people there is struggle.

Where there are strong people there is struggle

Where there is the spirit of our ancestors there is struggle.

Where there are intelligent minds there will be struggle.

Where there is like- minded people there will be struggle.

Where there is a very complex society and world, there will be struggle.

That is why "THE STRUGGLE NEVER ENDS"

THE FROG STORY

There were two frogs jumping in the woods, they jumped into a deep hole; the temperature began to drop and everything was freezing up. The two frogs were trying to jump out of the hole again and again they failed; the other frogs who were at the top of the hole shouted to the frogs in the hole, do not pain yourself with trying to get out, rest in peace. One of the frogs continued to jump until he jumps out of the hole. The frogs on the top of the hole asked the frog who jumped out, why did you continue to jump after we told you it was hopeless? The frog who had jumped out of the hole responded, I have a hearing problem, I thought you was saying jump harder. Words of wisdom #2 as long as there is life, "The struggle Never Ends."

Roger N. Toppin Sr.

2-10-2001

INVISIBLE CHAINS

There is a serious situation concerning Blacks here in America.

America is in a state of anxiety at the present time, due to the post Sept. 11, 2001 (911) syndrome. What does that have to do with this book or my title "The Struggle Never Ends"? After 911 the whole world changed. Money, which determines most peoples life or death, has become even scarcer. Yes, money is to power as health is to life style. In this book I will talk about Black folks, a lot of people will say here he goes again, with his Black thing.   Most of us figured we have it made in the main stream, think again we are in the process of being controlled confined and CHAINED again.   The slave chains were physical and we finally broke loose from them. The invisible chains, which remain, are psychological.   We as a people can break the invisible chains, using education information and determination.

THE PROBLEM

As Black people here in America for over 200 years, we remain the last hired and the first fired. We compose 12% of the population yet we have less than 1% of the businesses and property here in America. Black people are responsible for America being a successful society, yet we have very little input in policies, which will shape the future for the next generation. We must face the facts that percentage wise we have the highest numbers when it comes to: death, HIV/Aids, crime, bad health, poverty etc. Most of our children are not learning in school, they must steer clear of the drug culture. The criminal justice system is incarcerating our youth at a disproportionate rate. You are deprived of your right to vote if you are convicted of a felony, in turn we as a people loose some of our political power.

I recall reading a newspaper article from a Bronx, NY resident Ms. Josephine Dance, who stated (not her exact words) We are back in slavery, if your rights are taking away from you, when you are incarcerated, you are given a number, denied freedom, chained, and made to work for free etc. What Race has the most people incarcerated here in America?

SOLUTION:

Our number one priority should be EDUCATION, not just for Blacks but also for everyone here in America. People must come to realize that as long as there are inequities here in America, the world will fail to see America as the home of the brave and the land of the free. We have a great country, which is why almost everyone is coming here to live. We must educate others, and ourselves via schools, at work; at play everywhere, to the fact that you treat people the way you want to be treated.

Part of education, is knowing that if you are arrested for use or possession of illegal drugs your whole life can be screwed up. Being educated means you realize that one incident with drugs can mess you up for life, that is why educated / smart people stay away from drugs and people who use them. Over fifty percent of people incarcerated are in there for drugs, you do the math. There are plenty of ways to entertain yourself and others excluding the use of drugs.

We must pursue higher education for our families and ourselves; when it is practical. The more formal education you have, the more options you will have in life. Parents should keep in mind that the Board of Education cannot teach your children everything; you must take a part in the learning process. You must partner with your children's school, involving yourself in the Parent's Association etc. and remember your children are watching you for their role model, try to give them a positive image.

Money is very important with out it even an educated person will be in a hell of a position. I recall seeing a movie called "changing Places" staring Eddie Murphy, I think that movie should be used in schools, under economics 101, it had a great scenario about being broke (not having money). If you are educated / smart you will use your money wisely because money gives you options to decide your life style. The fact of the matter is the country is controlled by big money. I can go on and on but I do not want to make this subject a "War and Peace" book. I recommend that everyone work to make America the greatest country in the world, through self-improvement, and remember "The struggle Never Ends".

HEALTH

The year 2003 public announcements tells the public that annual physical examinations are not necessary and a waste of money.

Comment: I read report after report that early detection has saved thousands of people lives example: breast cancer and prostate cancer.

It appears that there is a conspiracy involving the health insurance companies and the news media.

Early detection will make the difference between whether you live or you die. Think about that.

Lung cancer is the number one cause of death with breast cancer being number two. I urge everyone to get an annual complete physical and medical exam from a physician. Early detection may save or prolong your life. You must remember that your life style plays an important part in your health. You have two or more very important reasons for keeping healthy the first is for yourself and the second is for your family. I wish you a long and healthy life.

STRUGGLE   HEALTH
WEIGHT PROBLEMS

1. It is in the mind!
2. Seniors / adults must be role models

3. You must have a goal

4. Children must start now

5. You must make choices

6. You must do some kind of physical exercise each day

7. You must change your whole lifestyle.

LEGAL DRUG MARKET

On Wednesday, November 6, 2003, I watched channel number 7, ABC, Night Line, Bill Koppel, who talked about the cost of legal drugs here in America, compared to the cost outside the USA, especially in Canada, where people are making trips and using the internet just to purchase their necessary prescriptions medications. Mr. Koppel asked an official from the FDA why couldn't the drug industry balance the price so Americans will be able to pay a fair price here in the USA. I think it is shame that so many Americans are put in this dilemma.

Hey wait a minute, we can't just say it is a shame; we must communicate with our elected officials and tell them to fix the problem.

UPDATE: Tuesday, December 8, 2003, Congress passed a so-called new drug prescription program bill, which the

President, Gorge W. Bush signed, into law. This new bill applies to Medicare members and will take effect in 2006.

Struggle, Economics

I made a visit to Providence, R.I. to spend some time with a friend.

I noticed that the community where I was staying was predominantly Hispanic; most of the community people spoke Spanish. The neighborhood was like a town in the Dominican Republic.

In the community there was a nightclub, a bodega, a restaurant, beauty shop, cleaners, auto repair, wholesale store, money order and money transfer store etc.

My main point is that in the community money circulates a long time before leaving. I want to also point out that most of the people are working in the community also live in the community.

Words of wisdom #3: The main Principle is spending your money where you can work.

Let me break it down for you, money makes the world go around. The news media reports we have a record high unemployment rates at the present time. After your health your money is the most important thing you have. Words of wisdom # 4, money will determine your life style, you must be a good money handler.

ECONOMICS 102

On Thursday, November 13, 2003, I was reading an article in the Amsterdam News. I will not mention names or exact locations to avoid embarrassment and other complications.

Awards were being given to outstanding Blacks and College Alumni at an Astoria Queens establishment. As I read the article, I reminisced about the many affairs I attended which had fabulous decorum and white waiters serving my every need. It is alleged that the establishments was owned and operated by organized crime people that was many years ago.and middle income Blacks have not woke up. We must keep the money in the family and community. I have heard the sad excuse that there are no nice places available in our community.

I say rent a community center and dress it up, hire Black waiters, to feed everyone and in the process you will feel more comfortable, when you eat the food. The accomplishments will be making employment for our people, while building up the community's economy. We must remember that " The Struggle Never Ends"

STRUGGLE-ECONOMICS TODAY

Today in America there is a two-tier system. I was looking at night line on channel number seven on Friday August 08, 2993, they was talking about the Hooker factory going out of business because china and other countries are making products cheaper and better. I had a discussion with a close friend who stated Black people make less money than white people who work side by side in North Carolina. The Blacks make less money because this is a holdover from slavery, when Blacks worked for free. Think about it here in America if a Black person makes a big complaint about the above system he or she will disappear and I do not mean magic.

NOV. 2003   Roger Toppin Sr.

"POST" (9/11)

(9/11) September 11, 2001

The world will never be the same after the 9/11 event. I will not go into the complete details of that day or its devastating effect on America in particular and the world in general. Most people in the world are now paranoid. If we have a black out the first thing on most people minds is it a terrorist act. People are now thinking short term; they want to live for today.

People are very insecure now and this situation will never change. We must accept the above facts and make the best out of a bad situation.

9/11 was the biggest event that America ever experienced, people confidence and sense of security have been shaken, knowing that we are now vulnerable to international terrorist attacks and conflicts.

I was going to vote at the poll, because it was Primary Day; and I was on the ballet running for city Council Member in the 12th district. I logged on to my computer and read a report that two airplanes had crashed into the World Trade buildings; my first reaction was that is a hell of a coincidence. I left my house and went to the poll; then I was informed that the election would be postponed until further notice, because city Hall was on emergency alert. As I listened to the news over the radios I realized that America was under attack. Like most people I started to communicate with family and friends to make sure they were safe.

In my mind, I began to realize that no place in the world is safe from international conflict not even in America. For the first week after the 9/11 attack people who had not spoken to me in years was now stopping to say hello. Big business was reaching out and offering special services and help to the tragedy; about a month later when the <u>life boat syndrome</u> had passed, people and businesses began to return to the dog eat dog mentality.

10-6-00

WE ARE INTERDEPENDENT

On Sunday November 2, 2003 I was reading the Oprah Magazine and to my surprise she admitted that in the past she was a very unsociable individual; but since she moved to a new home she has become a very sociable neighbor, which she states she really enjoys. I was thinking to myself here is a billionaire who just realized that no one is an island. I also read somewhere that people that interact with others socially, not only enjoy life, but live longer than people who are socially isolated or antisocial.

Words of wisdom #7:

It is in your best interest to interact with other people, especially people who are of like minds.

A CHAT AT LUNCH

On Tuesday, October 28, 2003, about 12:30 PM, I went to a senior lunch program in the co-op City community located in New York City, New York, the menu was chicken and rice and I was sitting at a table of about five people. The discussion of the proposed <u>87 billion</u> dollars the government wanted, to help rebuild Iraq came up. One gentleman stated I couldn't believe the government is talking about giving away that kind to money to another country with the conditions that exist here in New York City and America. He further stated don't they see all the homeless people who are out there and the soup lines, a lot of people are out of work and hurting badly. The majority of the people at the table were in full agreement with this gentleman.

I being an editor began to wonder how many other people are thinking this way. What are our congress representatives plans for that issue? It may be a good idea if the elected officials came by and had a lunch chat!

BLACK BURIAL GROUND IN NEW YORK CITY

On Sunday October 26, 2003 I was watching "Like It is" on Channel 7. The subject of the discussion was the re interment of the remains of African Americans "Blacks" which were discovered in 1991 in the Wall Street area, the remains were dug up for research. Some of the 400 or more bodies that were discovered during construction work in lower Manhattan. As always the issue of protocol as to who should be on the dais came up. All the politicians were up front, including New York City Mayor Michael Bloomberg, former Mayor David Dinkins, etc. A black speaker made it clear that if the officials came to honor the bodies of previous slaves they should help take people off welfare and provide employment, they should improve the educational system in the black community so that our children will have a better chance of being successful in adult life. The Black speaker stated Black slaves built New York City and Wall Street. A lot of them were worked to death including children.

Opinion: It was a very touching experience, observing the remains of our ancestors who made not only New York City, but also America an economic giant. The question of reparations should be a priority for this country, because you cannot go forward until you address the serious wounds inflicted on black people who were made to work for free as slaves. The souls of the dead as well as the souls of the living will rest easier, once America addresses and corrects this gross injustice of Blacks in history and the issue of reparation.

THE MASK!   NOV. 2003 R. TOPPIN SR.

BEING DIFFERENT

A lot of people want to be different which is great. If you are different in a positive way, you will be noticed while enhancing your quality of life. Being different, because you <u>do not</u> use illegal drugs, drink alcohol excessively, have unprotected sex, and other risky behavior. Remember there is only one of you, no clones, so live life to the fullest. You only have one life to live (smile).

Roger N. Toppin Sr.

STRUGGLE-THREE

nov. 2003

THINKING OUT LOUD

I log in on my computer today, Sunday, August 17, 2003; I saw a report, which states if you fix your dog with braces it will live longer. I was thinking to myself what if the government fixed poor citizens with braces, would that help save people lives. I believe in is a matter of priorities.

I was watching Gil Noble's "LIKE IT IS "today, Sunday, August 17, 2003; he interviewed Mr. Alton Maddox, a human rights attorney. Mr. Maddox stated that Black people were not included when the constitution was written; the writers of the Constitution considered Blacks as three fifth of a human being. Mr. Maddox wants the government to enforce the Amendments to the Constitution, especially the 13, 14, and 15.

PERSONAL COMMENT:

I hold Mr. Maddox in very high esteem, he was disbarred from practicing law because he championed causes of Blacks and other so called minorities. Mr. Maddox is still on the forefront of the human rights struggle. I urge everyone who believes in justice to support him and his cause; go a step further read the constitution of The United States, or at less the above mentioned amendments 13,14, and 15. Remember knowledge is power and "The Struggle Never Ends".

UPDATE: On Thursday, December 11, 2003 I purchased The New York Amsterdam News, and read an article called OPINION by Alton H. Maddox Jr. Who stated he had appealed to the appellate Court to be reinstated to practice law, he was denied. For thirteen years he has been barred from practice, because he apparently "disrespected" the system.

Maddox mentioned in his article that you could reach him: Alton H. Maddox Jr. 16 Court Street, Brooklyn, NY 11241. Telephone 1-718-834-9034.

Author's opinion, I read Mr. Maddox's article and said to myself this is one person who is of like-mind. Can you imagine being disbarred from practicing law for thirteen years; People have gone to jail for murder and came out in less time than that. I can reflect to Malcolm X before he was assassinated, no one wanted to be associated with him; they were afraid of being classified as pro Black. After Malcolm X's death almost everyone wanted to relate to what he represented, wearing clothes and jewelry with the letter X on it. The Federal Government gave him recognition by putting him on a United States postal stamp. Think about it we must support our freedom fighters when they need us the most, now.

Belated entry: On Thursday, August 17, 2003, the Northeast part of America and parts of Canada experienced **THE BIG BLACK OUT OF 2003**, the news media reported that this one was the biggest ever. I live in Co-op City, which is one of the nations biggest Cooperative developments. I will not go into the full details of this event but New York City along with the nation faired pretty well. Most people worked to make the situation bearable and there were no major reports of looting or violence. I listened to post comments from the people in the community, Who was thinking basically the same way example: At first I thought it was a terrorist attack, Why did it affect such a big part of the country, at Co-op City what happened to our back up emergency generators? We must prepare ourselves mentality and physically if this happens again. Some of the people, remembered the guidelines in "service Plus Newsletter" which I am the publisher / Editor; it is distribute in the community, bi- monthly free of charge. It is my opinion that the America people rallied together in this situation to make this country better.

BROWN VS. BOARD OF EDUCATION
"Topeka": 1954

The above case is about to have a <u>rerun</u>. We must study our history in order to protect our present and future position in this ...... society. Thurgood Marshall's efforts should not be in vain. With our united efforts we must stop the clock from being turned back.

BROWN VS. BOARD OF EDUCATION
UPDATE 2004

Monday, February 16, 2004. I watched TV channel 13, the documentary was about the town of Hoxie in Arkansas. There was a test case of separate but equal is not equal in education. In 1954 the Court found that Blacks and whites should attend the same schools, to comply with the 14 Amendment of the Constitution of The United States of America. The NAACP was involved in helping the transition.

Author's comments: A lot of people paid with their lives to make the landmark case a reality. There are people working to dismantle this important decision, we must stay vigilant and prevent the clock from being turned back. This year is the fiftieth anniversary of the US Supreme Court ruling Brown vs. The Board of Education. Never forget that "The Struggle Never Ends".

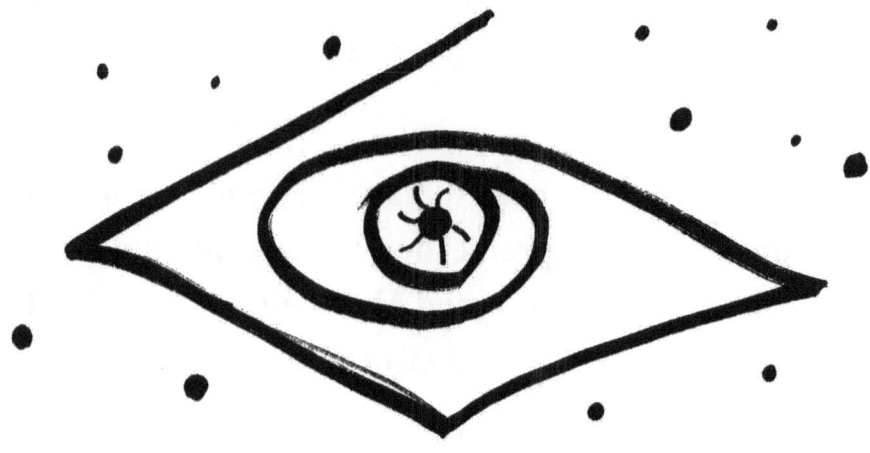

BiG BroTHER!   NOV. 2008   R. ToPPin SR.

NEWS-MEDIA

I want to address a very important issue that is the news media; most people do not realize how much it influences our lives. How much time do the average person spend in front of a TV set? Where do most people get their information? Who controls/owns the TV networks? I understand the government wants to allow networks to possess more than one TV and one radio station in a city or town. This will give certain people/ companies too much control over most people thinking process. We need checks and balances in place to prevent a possible brainwash.

There have been organizations that have been fighting the system for years to give Black people a more positive image on TV. A good case in point; I watched Whoopi Goldberg on channel 4, on Tuesday night, November 11, 2003. She had a scenario where the reporters interviewed her and some friends; when they looked at TV, the whole interview had been turned around in a very negative way. This is a very common practice. You must ask yourself who is reporting the story or issue and what interest do they have in its outcome.

Solution: Black people need to own and manage more News media establishments, example: TV programs "Like It Is", "Black Forum" Newspapers, "The Amsterdam News", The "The Daily Challenge" and "Service Plus Newsletter". There are many more positive Black news media, working to make America a better place for everyone and realize that "The Struggle Never Ends".

DRIVING WHILE BLACK

Yes, DWB is real! Most Black people know the real deal; this has been going on forever. Now the fact has been confirmed by New York City, channel nine, Brenda Blackman, who is a Black woman, spokesperson for that station.

I was watching the 10:00 P.M. news on Tuesday, November 18, 2003, which stated the TV station set up a test situation, were they had a Black male drive through a neighborhood in Nassau, and Long Island counties, there was a hidden camera recording the whole incident. The Black male was stopped questioned, handcuffed, searched and his auto was searched, after he informed the Police Officers he was lost, he was later released, because no crime or violation had been committed. This Black man's rights had been grossly violated.

The station also sent a white male into a very similar situation they did not report the results. The TV station confronted the Police commissioner who is Black, about receiving several complaints from other Blacks who stated they had similar experiences with the Police. The Police commissioner stated he would look into the matter. The TV station stated they would do a follow- up on the issue.

Opinion: I do not want people to think all Police officers are racist, because that is not the case. We have Brenda Blackman who is a Black woman and I would like to thank her publicly for a job well done. Brenda's report will help us work on some solutions.

We also have a Black Police commissioner, who must take the risk of doing the right thing. In this situation, I am not only a author but a former Police Officer / Community activist who realizes "The Struggle Never Ends'.

UPDATE: On Monday, December 7, 10:00 PM on channel nine. It was reported that the Black Police Commissioner in the above scenario received a derogatory letter, which was traced to a Police Benevolent Association member. This whole issue is now under investigation by several Government Agencies. It appears that a "Struggle Never Ends" part two may be necessary to keep up with this and many other important issues that are unfolding.

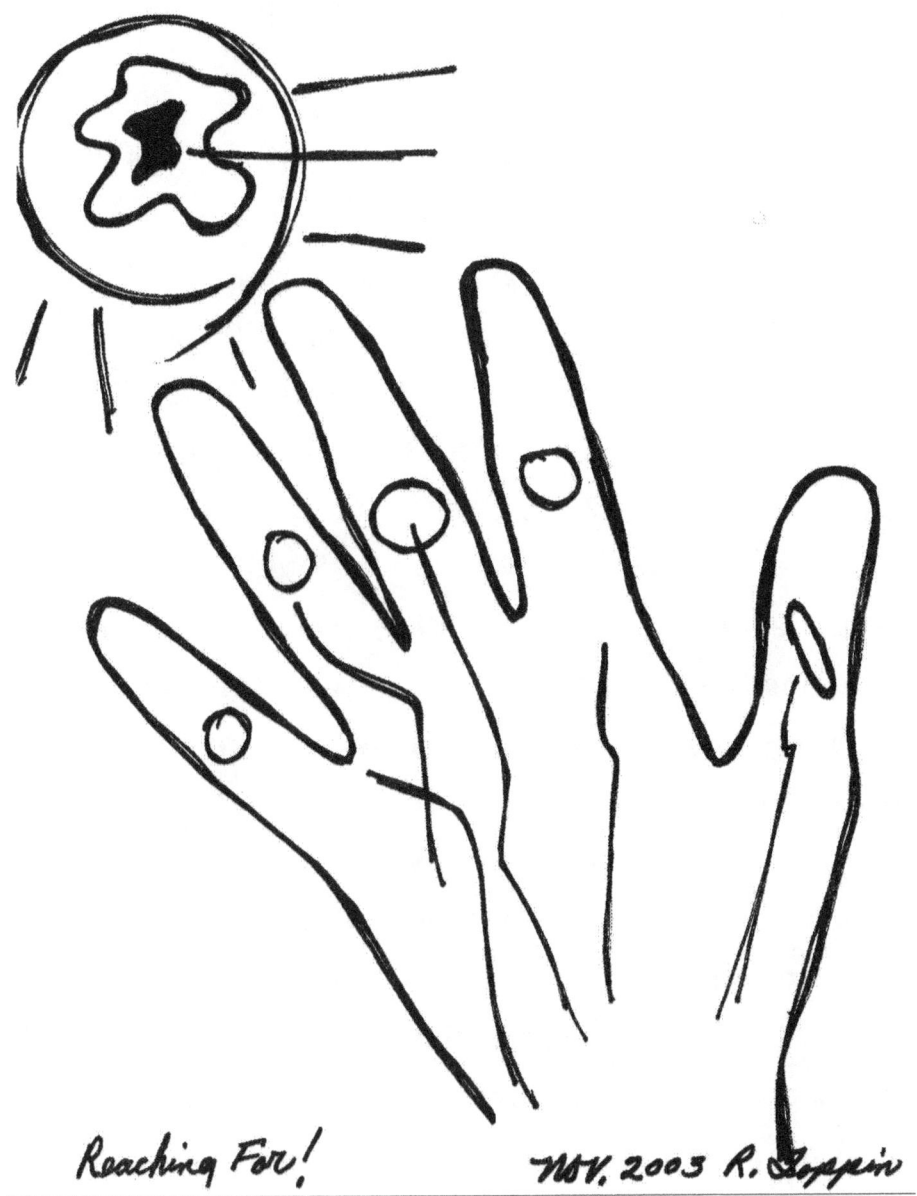

Reaching For!   Nov. 2003 R. Toppin

POSITIVE EXPERIENCE

I have been writing about a lot of negative things that have happen recently here in America; well I have great news, there are also positive things go on to. On Sunday November 23, 2003, I went to a fundraiser in the village of Harlem, sponsored by Sister's Uptown Bookstore LLC, located at 1492 Amsterdam Avenue, 156 Street. New York City, New York, Telephone 1-212-862-3680.

You may ask yourself why did I include New York after mentioning New York City? The answer is everywhere I go in the country there is a New York City, this and that etc. Back to my excursion, I drove to the Bookstore and to my surprise I found a parking space right away, if you live in New York City or visited here you would understand that was a small miracle in and of itself. I entered the establishment, I was informed that they were accepting donation to build a theater and expand their community programs, I was undecided if I should stay, when the receptionist offered to put a donation in for me, so I could say for the program, mentioning that she was a Christian and she wanted me to enjoy the program.

I was taken aback, thinking to myself that someone who did not know me would offer to put money up for me, here in New York City, I can not remember when that, has happen to me before. I refused the offer and put my own money up. I entered and received a program, which indicated the theme of the affair was "GATHERING OF AUTHORS". The mistress of ceremonies was verbalizing some poems with positive denotations and connotations about us (Black people) a female African-American drummer, who set the tone for a great affair, followed her.

I was thinking to myself I better use the men's room before I get pushed, I was thinking to myself everywhere you go in New York City, they tell you, they do not have bathrooms (toilets), I often think all these businesses and workers and no rest rooms (smile).

Back to my experience, I asked the proprietor where is the rest room and she directed me in the back, where I found a clean rest room with toilet paper and soap, do not laugh, this is rare in most establishments. There were refreshments, chicken, rice, Vegetables, dessert etc. the food was very good; the cooks did a great job.

After the food, a musical group named "Sojourner" consisting of four young ladies, two on the violin and one on the cello and one playing bass. They blew my mind away; never in my life did I hear such beautiful, exciting string music, at the end of their performance everyone gave them a standing ovation. I received one of their business cards: SOJOURNER telephone 1-718-205-6293 or www.sojourner-strings.com. I intend to see this group again. I recommend that anyone who want to witness this special musical phenomenon, get your tickets to their next affair.

I left the above affair thinking to myself, we experience and observe so many negative things happening in this world. This group of people and this day is one of many steps that move us as a people, to a higher level, and "The Struggle Never Ends".

UNITED NATION ASSOCIATION

Of the United States of America   On Friday, November 7, 2003 a friend, Ms. Priscilla Crowell, invited me (the Author) to a program at community Board 12 –Town Hall, located at 4101 White Plains Road, Bronx NY 10466, the theme of the program was "How Relevant is the United Nations to you? ". The interim officers were president Ms. Oneater Sinclair, vice Pres. Priscilla Crowell, Treasurer Betty Heyward, secretary Loretta Hassell, SSNYSD Board Member Bronx Adviser Thelma Dailey Atout, Members Lisa Dawson and Laura Rhodan. I arrived late (smile) According to the program Father Richard f. Gorman; Chairman NYC/ Bronx Community Board # 12 gave invocation and greetings

I came in to find the guest speaker Ms. Margaret K. Bruce who is a member of the United Nations Secretariat staff from its inception in 1945, giving everyone an overview of the Untied nations and its mission of trying to maintain peace in the world. The next speaker was Mr. John Figueroa, who is a student at Lehman College, representing a Model UN Program at Lehman College.

We had a dynamitic speaker Rev. Edward Colbert, Professor of Black Studies at Lehman College. Who stated he loves America, but we as Americans must reach out to the rest of the world, we are a small part of a bigger world that is changing, America cannot control the world forever. That is not word for word what was said, but a metaphor of what I was thinking. We had a presentation form Mr. Kenneth Mercer, executive Director of Edenwald Gunhill Neighborhood center, Inc. who pointed out that the next war might be over water and not oil.

The floor was opened up for questions from the audience, Ms. Joyce Howard pointed out that the United Nations have done a lot of positive things, feeding people, teaching people to read etc. During the Program refreshments were served, prepared by the above committee, you talk about some good food I ate a full plate and took some home.

I was informed that United Nations Association is looking for new members, for information contact the President, Ms. Oneater Sinclair, 3260 Cruger ave. Bronx, NY 10467 tel. 1-7118-798-5251.

I felt very good about the fact that dialogue concerning America and the world was taking place right here in the community. A lot of people might think or say, I have no voice or time for world events. The fact is each person is somebody and we all belong to one family and that is the human race. There were several young people at the above meeting, which is great because they must continue to take America in a positive direction and remember "The Struggle Never Ends".

A FIGHT FOR A BLACK WOMAN

There we go again, I received several e-mail messages in November of 2003, alleging a situation concerning, sister Shoshana Johnson a Black woman, who was in the army. She was taken as a prisoner during the war in Iraq, along with another female white soldier named Jessica Lynch, who was in the same unit along with some men. Shoshana was shot in both legs and traumatized. The Army came to the prisoners rescue and now the former prisoners are back in America.

It is alleged that Black Shoshana Johnson is getting unfair treatment and no recognition, compared to her white counterpart the white Jessica Lynch. It is also alleged that Ms. Lynch received 80% disability from the army, a movie and book contracts and wide media coverage. While Sister Johnson got 30% disability no movie or book contracts yet and very little media coverage.

All the above information is alleged, I do not have the necessary resources to confirm that the above story is true. One must be very careful when defending a Black woman, remember the Tawana case in New York State, where attorneys Alton Maddox, Vernon C. Mason and Reverend, Al Sharpton came to a Black woman's defense, and years later they are still paying the price with the attorneys being disbarred and their careers ruined.

Everyone was asked to contact his or her Congress Person and demand an investigation into the above matter. Shortly after receiving the above information I observed congressman Charlie Rangel on TV asking for the government to look into the above matter. I do not know the results, as of my writing this book, but I will continue to follow up on the above allegations, because " The Struggle Never Ends".

BLACK IS WHITE

Yes according to a recent DNA study Black (African-American) people who are Black in color can be considered White. Yes you read what I said correctly. The statement I made in a previous part of this book is true, "We all belong to one family the human race". I'm not making this up; I will give you my source.

On Friday, November 21, 2003, I was watching Night Line on TV Channel Seven. Chris Bostin, a spokesperson for the station was interviewing a Black man, I mean Black like me (dark black skin color). The black interviewee had a white mother. The Black man sent a blood sample to a notable DNA laboratory to find out his genetic heritage. The interviewee Black man was shocked to learn the results that stated he had no African-American genetics and was not considered Black or African- American by the scientific community. The Black man told several people that he was not Black or African-American, he was laughed at and told to get another test. The Black man stated that his whole life has been changed. He will put on the next census form that he is an American Native.

The Channel Seven spokesperson, consulted a specialist on DNA and genetics that stated the above scenario is very possible, and most people including white people will have some African- American or Black genetic traits, because Africa is the cradle of civilization.

Opinion: from the Editor, Roger N. Toppin Sr. I feel very sorry for the Black man who discovered he is not in the so called Black or Negroid race yet his skin color is Black.

I recall reading something by W.E.B. De Bois, who stated Black people had two consciences one white and one Black. If this Black man wants to maintain his sanity and continue to survive, here in America, he must continue his Black lifestyle and thinking. As I watched the discussion with the DNA / genetics specialist, I was thinking to myself this information reinforces what I learned years ago in my Black History studies. If we understand our history, work together on the present circumstances; we can make America better regardless of a person's race. In other words, "The Struggle Never Ends".

BELATED THANK YOU

To family and friends who were and still are a part of my life and the foundation of this book. "THE STRUGGLE NEVER ENDS".

The late Robert Westley Durham and the Late Joan O. Rahman. The above named people were real icons in the community who never were really recognized. We must remember that the real freedom fighters will never be recognized by a negative system and the local news media. As is the case, all the house Blacks will be advertised in the news media while in the real world these people only represent their self and their bosses. Let me get back to the positive people in the struggle.

Delores, Devante, Eric Jr. Janet, Penny, Surggie, Charles, Betty, Anna Belle, Thomas, Larry, Antoinette, Gladys, Arthur, La Shawn, Tenisha, Bill, Marvin, Pete, Julie, Ben, Ronnie, Mildred, Edith, Ethel, Raymond, Ann, Kenny, Thelma, Pat, Jamie, Hattie, Judy, Gloria, Chink, Sonny, Harold, James, Terry, Cal, Jose, Simpson, Brenda, Mary, Robert, Henry, Regina, Virginia, Ted, Harmon, Roger, Bea, Margie, Shirley, Rodney, James, Maxine, Elaine, Joyce, Arthur, Stewart,

Lenny, Joan, Evelyn, George, Francine, Janet, Elizabeth, Susan, Louise, Gladys, Stephanie, Geri, Kojo, Randolph, Carolyn, Lizzie, Jennifer, Othelia, Clarence, Sylvester, Hazel, Leonard, Divine, Carolyn, Mitch, Henry, Ruth, Paul, Marie, Donald, Doris, Carrie, Mary, Bill, Artie, Margie, Margaret, Tommy, Lalie, Butch, Billy, Bob, Richard, Cephus, Marlene, William, Melvin, Eleanor, Joel, Bertha, Toni, Ora, Rita, Eddie, Raymond, Alan, Jenette, Donna, Aubrey, Kenneth, Mena, Rose, Esther, Charisse, Christeen, Jean, Geneva, Edna, Fred, Earl, Willie, Willis, Jr. Kim, Tim, Mark, Ronald, Beverly, Ermitt, Ruth, Jippy, Regina, Doreen, Crystal, Tillye, Ardy, Sam, Baruti, Cynthia, Calvin, Alma, Mat, Jennie, Dorothy, Junior, Luther, Doc, Carmen, Catherine, Bill, Burnie, Mich, Lottie, Oneater, Priscilla, Loretta, Lisa, Laura, Joe, Iris, Al, Barry, Big Paul and many, many more who I can not remember at this time.

BELATED THANK YOU 2

I was thinking of people of like-mind and the name Eric Adams, Co-Founder, of 100 Blacks in Law Enforcement who Care, came to mind. His style and positions remind me of myself back in the day. I never met him, I only read about the stands he and his organization has taken. It appears that given a chose of being Black or blue he choose to work for and stand with the Community. I know from first hand experience that taking a positive position can and will get you in hot water. The Community must remember if you truly support and stand up for truth and justice, you will became a target; therefore we must be prepared to defend and support individuals who have our best interests at heart.

Recently November 2003, there was a question on the ballot concerning Nonpartisan elections, which was defeated, Eric Adams, supported it, giving the reason, Nonpartisan elections give candidates and votes more opportunity to focus on the important issues confronting New York City. Why bring up the issue if it was defeated? Because history is very important, and we will be confront again with a similar issue, in a different format in the near future!

Opinion: As a former City Council Member candidate, I must agree with Eric Adams on this issue. Black people should not be in the back pocket of any party or individual, we have been taken for granted too long. Black should not have permanent friends or enemies' only permanent positive interests, because the "Struggle Never Ends".

AMERICA'S DEBT

This passage pertains to REPARATIONS FOR BLACKS. On Wednesday, December 3, 2003, I was looking at Night Line on TV. Channel seven; Spokesperson, John Donvan presented " America in Black and White".

The program told it like it is! He was interviewing a woman concerning the Slave Policy, The interviewee stated she had family and friends who were slaves in 1960's, and they worked without getting paid.

The slavery policy involved a lot of big companies that are in business today. The TV program not me (smile) mention Brown Brothers, Fleet Bank, J.P. Morgan Bank and many others. It was also pointed out that Washington DC was built by slaves.

A white lawyer, who is representing Black people, states Blacks should use the court of public opinion, like the holocaust victims did, to get money from German and Swiss banks / companies. There is a pending law suit concerning the above issue, in Chicago.

There was pro and con discussion about this issue, including a few Blacks who stated, we should forget about this issue and move on. The author's opinion is Black people should be treated like everyone else. The money could be used to build educational facilities for the next generation of Blacks, who great grand parents built the foundation of America for free.

The book "The Debt" what America Owns Blacks, by Randall Robinson was mention, during the interview, I recommend you read it.

HISTORY LESSON

It is Saturday, December 6, 2003. The time is 8:00 PM, and I am snowbound in my apartment. What to do? I looked at the TV program and decided to watch "Rosewood" directed by John Singleton 1997, on channel 11.

This was a true story that took place in Rosewood, Florida, in 1923. I had seen the movie previously, but I wanted to reinforce my thoughts on this very serious documentary. I also had previous thoughts of including this information in my book "The Struggle Never Ends" but I though in was to old, to be of interest. After watching the movie I felt that this is a very important history lesson.

We must critique the scenario and the plot involved in this documentary. We have a town where Black and White people live. Co-existing in a delicate environment. A white girl ALLEGES that a Black boy raped her, which leads to the beginning of a Black holocaust. I will not go into the ugly details that follow.

You may say to yourself, why is he bringing this old news up now. History repeats itself. I recall reading about a similar

Black holocaust that happened in Tulsa, Oklahoma (Black Wall Street) about the same time as "Rosewood". I can recall back in the 1960s, a black boy whistled at a white woman in the South and he was killed. Again you may say this is 2003. I recall a Black supreme court Judge, Clarence Thomas used the term "High Tech Lynching".

Recently we had a case involving a professional athlete, accused of rapping a white girl, what are the odds he will be found innocent? My point is, the same game but a different name. Remember he/she who does not analyze history will repeat it. I recommend you read the book or see video " Rosewood" by John Singleton. Take your knowledge to a higher level. I know you are smart that is why you are reading my book.

THANKSGIVING?

I just finished sharing a special thanksgiving dinner, with family members and friends. It was great. I am relaxing watching BET Aretha Franklin Walk of Fame Special on TV.

I know you are thinking to yourself; were is he going with this passage. I started to reflect on a TV program I watched this past Sunday. "Like It Is " Gil Noble was the narrator who was interviewing an American Indian, who is a social worker with a master's degree in sociology. Her tribe lives in Massachusetts.

The interviewee explained that her people the American Indians are still suffering from the after affects of being make to live on a reservation, and giving up many of their customs that were passed down from their ancestors. She mentions the fact that germ warfare was used against her people, when they were given blankets which contained yellow fever germs. She also stated that her people are still struggling to survive in a country that displaced them.

The next day (Monday) I ran into a friend of mine who is white, Harriet Silver, I wished her a happy holiday, she stopped and explained we are celebrating a day that we displaced and infected with yellow fever the American Indians. America should be shame of what we did. I asked her did she see "Like It Is " on TV, she stated no. I thought to myself what a coincidence. I was thinking to myself there are a lot of people who know the real history of Thanksgiving.

I called my sister and asked her if she had any plans for the holiday, she said yes, I am going upstate to share time and food with the American Indians on the reservation.

I was thinking why spoil a great day, when families are spending time together and are enjoying life. The fact is we must look history in the face and admit our misgivings; we must make some concessions. God Bless America!

UPDATE: On Monday, December 8, 2003. I read an article in the New York Times. It stated the dogrib Indians would receive 152 million Canadian dollars and Diamonds royalties in Ottawa, Canada. This is part of a settlement for claims for their ancestral lands. This is only part of 1.6 billion Canadian dollars or $ 1.2 billion American dollars that the Indians will receive. This money will be divided among 16 groups. There are another 62 land claims pending. Author's opinion this is what I call doing the right thing. Belated, Happy Thanksgiving to those Indians involved.

Rozn Lppin Jr   7·22·00

POLICE BEAT MAN TO DEATH

I was thinking to myself keep quiet about this incident. Why become a target. I was feeling very stressed. I was thinking to myself, I must be prepared to pay the price for telling the truth. I gave it some thought and decided to write this article, life is full of dangers. Our ancestors had to stand up to the system in order to make life better for us and now it is our responsibility to struggle to make life better for the next generation.

Here I go, on Monday, December 1, 2003, I watched TV and was shocked to observe the Police beating a Black man to death.

The story was reported like this. On Sunday, November 30, 2003, in Cincinnati, the Police had videotaped an incident, where it is alleged a Black unarmed man attacked them. The two white Police Officers alleged to use necessary force, wielding their nightsticks to subdue the now dead victim / perpetrator. It is alleged Nathaniel Jones, a Black 350 pounds male, had a trace of drugs in his system. Later it was shown on a separate video that Nathaniel Jones was in a restaurant and displayed so called bazaar activity. The EMS was called, but somehow the police became involved at which time the EMS left. This reminds me of the Eleanor Bumpbers case, where a mentally distraught person was treated like a criminal and was shot to death.

Why is it I ask myself that this happens time and time again to Black persons? How are others that display bazaar actions treated. Is this selective telecasting, or are Blacks the only victims to be treated in this manner? Cut up videos blown across the Television screen over and over again, as if to brainwash us, and any facts that bring a question to the procedure are quickly dropped and only the beating of the victim is shown.

The Mayor of the Cincinnati stated, the videotape showed that the Police Officers were justified, in the outcome of the above incident. As an Editor, former Police Officer and Community activist, this incident does not sit right with me.

The public needs to know the when, where, who, what, why and how of this incident. I want to see an investigation conducted by outside agencies, such as the State and Federal investigational Departments and the results made public.

Some people may think it is hopeless, but it is not hopeless. We the people must demand respect and justice and remember "The Struggle Never Ends".

UPDATE: On Thursday, December 11, 2003, I read The New York Amsterdam News which, alleged most of the news media had reported prior to the Police Department responding to the scene, where Nathaniel Jones was confronted. He was dancing in a restaurant.

The videotape recovered from the restaurant showed the victim Jones doing exercise and doing calisthenics; he was not doing anything illegal. He did not have a weapon. This appears to follow the pattern of discrediting most victims to justify questionable Police actions.

You may ask yourself why is he writing about this incident. The answer is we see this scenario happening over and over again to our people. I am thinking that could have happen to me; or someone in my family.

"THE STRUGGLE NEVER ENDS"

I live in Co-op City, which is the biggest Co-op project in the State of New York. At the present time August 2003 the development is in a state of flux. There is a outstanding large mortgage, a huge problem with the garages that are in disrepair due to poor construction and poor maintenance The windows need to be replaced they are over 30 years old. The Present Board of Directors claims to be investigating which direction to take the development in order to stabilize it. The two main options are <u>Privatization</u> in which shareholders will be able to sell their apartments at a big profit but the people who remain will pay a huge rent increase. We have the option of remaining in the <u>Mitchell- Lama Program</u> in which we will receive huge tax breaks assistance from the State, subsidizes for low-income people who are using them at the present time.

CO-OP CITY, A CITY WITHIN NEW YORK CITY

Today is Thursday, December 25, 2003, this is an update of a very serious issue, affordable housing, which is on the top of most people's priority list. Hopefully this is the final part of "The Struggle Never Ends" first edition. Will there be a " The Struggle Never Ends" second edition? The answer to that question is in the hands of the people who read the first edition! I apologize for going off the subject of Co- op City.

I live in a place called Co-op City; before I arrived I read about the struggle where the late, President of the NAACP Ms. Laura Valdes, who was an attorney took Riverbay Corp to court and made them start accepting, the so called minorities in the development. I have lived there for 20 years. It is a city within a city, a Mitchell-Lama development that was flirting with becoming a Privatized Housing development. A garage crisis (the closing of four garages at one time, because of dangerous conditions) forced the present Riverbay Board of Directors to sit down with the State and come up with a new agreement, within the Mitchell- Lama Program.

Let's back up to the beginning of Riverbay Corporation/ Co-op City, which was built on a tract of land formerly known as Freedom land an entertainment enterprise. The building of the development started about May 1966; It includes a power plant, fire house, Public Safety station, several schools, Churches, and community organizations.The State and City came together to provide affordable housing for middle – income people. There are about 55,000 people living in the development.

There is legislation in Albany, New York A.2367 (Lopez) which would extend from 20 years to 50 years the period of time before limited-profit housing companies may dissolve and leave the Mitchell- lama program. Co-op City may receive ½ billion dollars from the State for major improvements and upgrades.

My living twenty years in the same place tells you something about how I feel about Co-op City, There are many more problems that need to be addressed, the cause of the above crisis who is responsible? People must be held accountable for their action or inactions. This is big business, with the shareholders voting for people who will have their best interests at heart. There is a bright future for co=op City, but we must work together to make it happen. If you looking for a great deal in today market this is the place.

CO-OP CITY UPDATE

Riverbay corporation Board of Directors and New York State Housing Finance Agency (HFA) have come to an agreementsubjecttoapprovalbythecooperators/shareholders in a referendum. The agreement is to borrow $475,000,000 dollars for the capital improvement projects such as garages and balconies. The vote is scheduled for Tuesday, March 16, 2004. There will be an election for the Riverbay Board of Directors on June 2004. The above factors will determine the future of Co-op City and the community.

Update: On Tuesday, March 16, 2004, the cooperators voted yes to the above referendum!

"THE STRUGGLE NEVER ENDS"

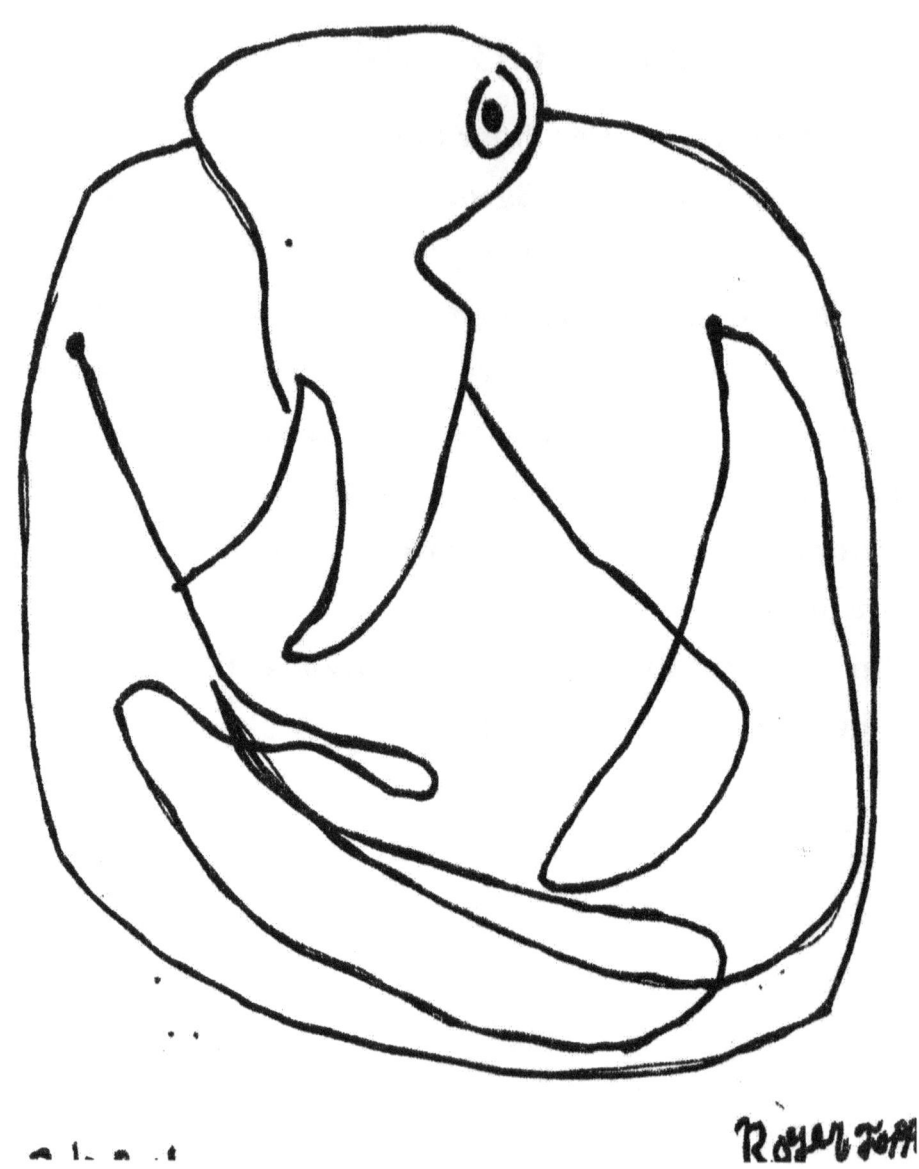

A DISCUSSION WITH MY SON

Today is Monday December 15, 2003. I thought it would be a very good thing to get a brief statement from my son Roger Toppin, Jr., who is now 17 years old.

<u>Roger Sr.</u> My question to him was when you read the outline of the book "The Struggle Never Ends", what was your thoughts on America's past, present and future. His remarks

<u>Roger Jr.</u> "Black people have a tough time fitting in. If I am assigned to the draft, then I'll have to risk my life for America of course. I'm hoping for the future to be better. We should try to live in harmony with the rest of the world. We should pray for world peace."

<u>Roger Sr.</u> I thanked him for his time and thoughts and told him to go to bed. In order to have a clear mind, to prepare for the future!

A DISCUSSION WITH MY SON (PART 2)

Today is Sunday December 21, 2003. Previously I had a discussion with my son, Roger Toppin Jr., which was very brief. Today I want to expand on my son's thoughts and ideas about America.

<u>Roger Sr.</u> My son said,"

<u>Roger Jr.</u> People get upset when Black men date white women" Everybody should be allowed to date anyone regardless of their race. If I'm drafted, then I will have no other choice but to go to war. We should have Peace rather than war.

<u>Roger Sr.</u> I then ask my son what he thought about the future of America. He stated,

<u>Roger Jr.</u> " I'm optimistic that America will have a better future. In the future, I think that we will need more support for Senior Citizens, Children and homeless people.

<u>Roger Sr.</u> what would be the first thing you would do if you became President of the United States of America?

<u>Roger Jr.</u> If I were President of the USA the first thing I would do is help all the homeless people. Second thing I would do is help clean up America.

<u>Roger Sr</u>. Even if you do not become president of the United States of America, you should still pursue your goals.

<u>Roger Jr</u>. My dad said even if I don't become President of the USA that I could still work on the above issues.

<u>Roger Sr</u>. thank you, this is your world, so prepare to handle it.

THE FEAR OF HISTORY

I wanted to leave this subject alone, after reading about it and seeing jokes about it on TV, I would be remiss not to include this bit of history, in my book. This particular scenario is still playing out and effecting people lives today. This is a case in point, that "The Struggle Never Ends". By now you are saying to yourself, what in the hell is he talking about?

I am talking about the <u>alleged allegation</u> from Mrs. Essie Mae Washington-Williams, who is a Black 78 years old retired teacher who lives in Los Angeles, California. Ms. Washington-Williams stated she is the daughter of the late senator, Strom Thurmond who was white. Ms. Washington-Williams, also stated she is "completely free" now that she revealed the truth. According to an article in the New York Times, dated Saturday, December 20, 2003.

Mr. Thurmond was <u>alleged</u> to be a staunch segregationist; he died at the age of 100 in June 2003. It is <u>alleged</u> that in South Carolina Ms Washington-Williams mother was a Black 15 years old maid, at the time working in the Thurmond's household when the affair took place.

The New York Times alleged, that the Thurmond family was struggling with the above information.

Author's opinion: I can understand a little, how Ms. Washington-Williams felt because I was a little up tight about writing the <u>alleged</u> story. Imagine walking around with fear of the truth getting out all those years. In a previous part of this book I mentioned "The Invisible Chains" that is what happen here. We are still living in fear of the truth, Black people and white people. In order for America to move forward and everyone to free their minds and souls we must face the truth. In our hearts most people know the truth about America's history.

Roger Toppin. 72

OUR LEGACY

When you write, draw, record or produce music, you are recording a time of our presence here on earth. We learned about our foreparents and the world events from books, pictures, movies, music, and elder-brain banks etc. from previous documentation. It is our responsibility to leave documents, which will include an outline of this complex society and our time here on earth. We must teach the next generation; that the "Struggle Never Ends".

FOCUS

FOCUS

FOCUS

AND REMEMBER THAT

"THE STRUGGLE NEVER ENDS"

" THE STRUGGLE NEVER ENDS"

AUTHOR'S PROFILE

ROGER N. TOPPIN, Sr., Author of "The Struggle Never Ends" was born in New York City, New York, on December 31, 1935 I am divorced with three boy children. I spent most of my adult life in the Borough of the Bronx. Throughout my lifetime I was always very involved in the social/political process of America.

I ran the gamut from teenage gang President to Political Club president. I am still involved with empowering the community and preparing our youth for tomorrow's struggles.

I have designed this book as a <u>blueprint</u> for people who are like-minded and realize that "The Struggle Never Ends" I served four years in the U.S. Navy as a sailor, worked for the Department of Hospitals, as a Hospital Aide, worked for the NYC Housing Authority in the maintenance Department, New York City Police Department, as a Police officer, Served as President of Public School Parent's Association (160) in the Bronx, worked for the Board of Education, as a School Aide, worked for the U.S. Postal Service, as Mail carrier, I served as President of the African–American Association, of Co-op City which is located in New York City, served as President of Harriet Tubman Democratic club of Co-op City, located in New York City, I am presently the Publisher / Editor of "Service Plus Newsletter" which is distributed in Co-op City and the New York City communities..

Roger Hoppin Jr.   12-2000